MW00368252

Call of the Wild

Call of the Wild

Quotes from the Great Outdoors

RUNNING PRESS

PHILADELPHIA · LONDON

A Running Press® Miniature Edition™
©2002 by Running Press

All rights reserved under the Pan-American and International
Copyright Conventions

Printed in China

*This book may not be reproduced in whole or in part, in any form or by
any means, electronic or mechanical, including photocopying, recording,
or by any information storage and retrieval system now known or here-
after invented, without written permission from the publisher.*

The proprietary trade dress, including the size and format, of this
Running Press® Miniature Edition™ is the property of Running Press.
It may not be used or reproduced without the express written
permission of Running Press.

Library of Congress Cataloging-in-Publication Number: 2002100727

ISBN: 0-7624-1359-X

This book may be ordered by mail from the publisher. Please include
$1.00 for postage and handling. ***But try your bookstore first!***

Running Press Book Publishers
125 South Twenty-second Street
Philadelphia, Pennsylvania 19103-4399

Log onto www.specialfavors.com to order Running Press®
Miniature Editions™ with your own custom-made covers!

Visit us on the web!
www.runningpress.com

Through woods and
mountain passes
The winds, like
anthems, roll.

—Henry Wadsworth Longfellow
(1807–1882)
American poet

5

Keep not standing,
   fixed and rooted,
Briskly venture,
   briskly roam.

—Johann Wolfgang von Goethe
            (1749–1832)
      German writer

Nature never
did betray the heart
that loved her.

—William Wordsworth
(1770–1850)
British poet

8

Men argue;
Nature acts.

—Voltaire
(1694–1778)
French writer and philosopher

Look deep into nature,
and then you
will understand
everything better.

—Albert Einstein
(1879–1955)
German-born physicist

11

Give me a spark
of Nature's fire.
That's all the
learning I desire.

—Robert Burns
(1759–1796)
Scottish poet

12

Nature understands
her business
better than we do.

—Michel de Montaigne
(1533–1592)
French essayist

I went to the woods because
I wished to live deliberately,
to front only the essential
facts of life, and see if I
could not learn what
it had to teach, and not,
when I came to die,
discover that I had not lived.

—Henry David Thoreau
(1817–1862)
American writer and philosopher

Eventually, all things
merge into one, and a
river runs through it.
The river was cut by the
world's great flood and

runs over rocks from the basement of time. On some of the rocks are timeless raindrops. Under the rocks are the words, and some of the words are theirs. I am haunted by waters.

—Norman Maclean
(1902–1990)
American writer

Nature does nothing uselessly.

—Aristotle
(384–322 B.C.)
Greek philosopher

People from a planet
without flowers
would think we must
be mad with joy
the whole time to have
such things about us.

—Iris Murdoch
(1919–1999)
British writer

21

The sky above blankets me. The fire I build warms me. The food I pick nourishes me. And that is all I ever need.

—Jane Goodall
British wildlife researcher

24

Society speaks and
all men listen,
mountains speak
and wise men listen.

—John Muir
(1838–1914)
American naturalist

Great things
are done when
men and
mountains meet.

—William Blake
(1757–1827)
British poet and artist

27

To the dull mind,
nature is leaden.
To the illuminated
mind the whole
world burns and
sparkles with light.

—Ralph Waldo Emerson
(1803–1882)
American essayist and poet

30

Nature, like man,
sometimes weeps
from gladness.

—Benjamin Disraeli
(1804–1881)
British prime minister

I think that I shall never see
A poem as lovely as a tree
A tree whose hungry mouth is
    pressed
Against the earth's sweet flowing
    breast . . .
Poems are made by fools like me,
But only God can make a tree.

—Joyce Kilmer
(1886–1918)
American poet

We do not inherit
the earth from
our ancestors.
We borrow it
from our children.

—Haida Indian saying

And April weeps—but,
O ye hours!
Follow with May's fairest
flowers.

—Percy Bysshe Shelley
(1792–1822)
British poet

35

Now I see the secret
of making the
best person: it is to
grow in the open
air and to eat and
sleep with the earth.

—Walt Whitman
(1819–1892)
American poet

I'd rather wake up in the middle of nowhere than in any city on earth.

—Steve McQueen
(1930–1980)
American actor

Then here's a hail to
   each flaming dawn,
And here's a cheer to
   the night that's gone,
And may I go a roam-
   ing on,
Until the day I die.

—Carved into a rock on
Mount Katahdin, Maine

Nothing is more
beautiful than the
loveliness of the
woods before sunrise.

—George Washington Carver
(1864–1943)
American educator
and agricultural scientist

42

I was born upon thy bank,
   river,
My blood flows in thy
   stream,
And thou meanderest
   forever
At the bottom of my dream.

—Henry David Thoreau
     (1817–1862)
American writer and philosopher

One touch of nature
makes the
whole world kin.

—William Shakespeare
(1564–1616)
British playwright and poet

46

I like trees because they
seem more resigned to
the way they have to live
than other things do.

—Willa Cather
(1873–1947)
American writer

The Sun, the hearth
of affection and life,
pours burning love on
the delighted earth.

—Arthur Rimbaud
(1854–1891)
French poet

Deviation from
nature is deviation
from happiness.

—Samuel Johnson
(1709–1784)
British writer

Who can ever
express
the ecstasy of
the woods?

—Ludwig van Beethoven
(1770–1827)
German composer

The clearest way
into the universe
is through a
forest wilderness.

—John Muir
(1838–1914)
American naturalist

In wilderness I sense
the miracle of life,
and behind it our
scientific accomplish-
ments fade to trivia.

—Charles Lindbergh
(1902–1974)
American aviator

54

Rest is not idleness, and to lie
sometimes on the grass
under trees on a summer's day,
listening to the murmur
of water, or watching the clouds
float across the sky,
is by no means a waste of time.

—Sir John Lubbock
(1834–1913)
British banker, statesman, and naturalist

You have to leave the city
of your comfort and
go into the wilderness
of your intuition. What
you'll discover will be
wonderful. What you'll
discover will be yourself.

—Alan Alda
American actor,
director, and writer

I believe in God,
only I spell it nature.

—Frank Lloyd Wright
(1867–1959)
American architect

Big Blue Mountain Spirit,
The home made of blue
clouds . . .
I am grateful for that way
of goodness there.

—Apache chant

There is not in the wide
world a valley so sweet
As that vale in whose bosom
the bright waters meet

—Thomas Moore
(1779–1852)
Irish poet

All journeys have a
secret in which the
traveler is unaware.

—Martin Buber
(1878–1965)
Austrian philosopher
and theologian

As the leaves of
the trees are said
to absorb all
noxious qualities
of the air, and
to breathe forth
a purer atmos-
phere, so it
seems to me as
if they drew from

us all sordid and angry passions,
and breathed forth peace and
philanthropy. There is a severe
and settled majesty in woodland
scenery that enters into the soul,
and dilates and elevates it,
and fills it with noble inclinations.

—**Washington Irving**
(1783–1859)
American writer

What is my fleeting
existence in comparison
with that decaying rock,
that valley digging its
channel ever deeper, that
forest that is tottering and
those great masses above
my head about to fall?

—Denis Diderot
(1713–1784)
French philosopher and writer

What is there in thee, Moon!
that thou should'st move
My heart so potently?

—John Keats
(1795–1821)
British poet

Earth's crammed with
    heaven,
And every common bush
    afire with God;
But only he who sees,
    takes off his shoes—
The rest sit round it and
    pluck blackberries.

—Elizabeth Barrett Browning
        (1806–1861)
        British poet

A single sunbeam is
enough to drive
away many shadows.

—St. Francis of Assisi
(1182–1226)
Patron Saint of Animals
and Ecology

73

Where there is
sunshine,
there is also shade.

—Kashmiri proverb

I often think that the night is more alive and more richly colored than the day.

—Vincent van Gogh
(1853–1890)
Dutch artist

There is something
haunting in the
light of the moon; it has
all the dispassionateness
of a disembodied soul,
and something of its
inconceivable mystery.

—Joseph Conrad
(1857–1924)
Polish-born English writer

All my life through,
the new sights of
nature made me
rejoice like a child.

—Marie Curie
(1867–1934)
Polish scientist

No matter how sophisticated you may be, a large granite mountain cannot be denied—it speaks in silence to the very core of your being.

There are some that love
not to listen but the
disciples are drawn to the
high altar with magnetic
certainty, knowing that a
great Presence hovers over
the ranges.

—Ansel Adams
(1902–1984)
American photographer

Thou hast a voice, great
   Mountain, to repeal
Large codes of fraud and
   woe; not understood
By all, but which the wise,
   and great, and good
Interpret, or make felt,
   or deeply feel.

—Percy Bysshe Shelley
      (1792–1822)
      British poet

Who has seen the wind?
Neither you nor I:
But when the trees bow
   down their heads,
The wind is passing by.

—Christina Rosetti
  (1830–1894)
  British poet

I grew up in this town, my poetry was born between the hill and the river, it took its voice from the rain, and like the timber, it steeped itself in the forests.

—Pablo Neruda
(1904–1973)
Chilean poet and diplomat

The sun, with all those
planets revolving around
it and dependent on it,
can still ripen a bunch of
grapes as if it had nothing
else in the universe to do.

—Galileo
(1564–1642)
Italian astronomer and physicist

I sat in silent musing—
The soft wind waved my hair;
It told me heaven was glorious
And sleeping earth was fair.

—Emily Brontë
(1818–1848)
British writer

When you take a flower
in your hand and
really look at it, it's your
world for the moment.
I want to give that
world to someone else. I
want them to see it whether
they want to or not.

—Georgia O'Keeffe
(1887–1986)
American artist

A bird does not
sing because it has
an answer.
It sings because
it has a song.

—Chinese proverb

No bird soars too high,
if he soars
with his own wings.

—William Blake
(1757–1827)
British poet and artist

Those who contemplate
the beauty of the
earth find reserves of
strength that will
endure as long as life lasts.

—Rachel Carson
(1907–1964)
American zoologist and writer

The winds of grace
blow all the time.
All we need to
do is set our sails.

—Ramakrishna
(1836–1886)
Indian spiritualist

101

We live
in a rainbow
of chaos.

—Paul Cézanne
(1839–1906)
French artist

Up high all the birds have
    flown away,
A single cloud drifts off
    across the sky.
We settle down together,
    never tiring of each other,
Only the two of us,
    the mountain and I.

—Li Po
8TH century Taoist poet

Perhaps the truth
depends on a walk
around the lake.

—Wallace Stevens
(1879–1955)
American poet

Mountains are
earth's
undecaying
monuments.

—Nathaniel Hawthorne
(1804–1864)
American writer

108

I prefer winter and fall, when you feel the bone structure of the land-scape—the loneliness of it—the dead feeling of winter. Something waits beneath it—the whole story doesn't show.

—Andrew Wyeth
American artist

We have nothing to fear and a great
deal to learn from trees,
that vigorous and pacific tribe which
without stint produces strengthening
essences for us, soothing balms,
and in whose gracious
company we spend so many cool,
silent, and intimate hours.

—Marcel Proust
(1871–1922)
French writer

113

The face of the water, in time, became a wonderful book—a book that was a dead language to the uneducated passenger, but which told its mind to me without reserve, delivering its most cherished secrets as clearly as if it uttered them with a voice. And it was not a book to be read once and thrown aside, for it had a new story to tell every day.

—Mark Twain
(1835–1910)
American writer and humorist

Water, everywhere over
the earth, flows to join
together. A single natural law
controls it. Each human
is a member of a community
and should work within it.

—The *I Ching*

In the depth of winter,
I finally learned
that within me there lay
an invincible summer.

—Albert Camus
(1913–1960)
French writer

I walk without flinching
through the burning
cathedral of the summer.
My bank of wild grass is
majestic and full of music.
It is a fire that solitude
presses against my lips.

—Violette Leduc
(1907–1972)
French writer

In all things of
nature there
is something of
the marvelous.

—Aristotle
(384–322 B.C.)
Greek philosopher

120

I think ever again my
small adventures,
My fears, those small ones
that seemed so big,
For all the vital things
I had to get and reach;

And yet there is only one
   great thing,
The only thing
To live to see the great day
   that dawns
And the light that fills the
   world.

—19TH century
Inuit Native American

Photography Credits

© Carr Clifton: front cover and pp. 16–17, 25, 28–29, 49, 53, 56–57, 61, 74–75, 78–79, 102, 124–125

© Kathleen Norris Cook: back cover and pp. 6, 13, 22–23, 44–45, 64–65, 70–71, 84–85, 95, 98–99, 110–111, 121

Joe Cornish, © Digital Vision: pp. 2, 9, 18, 33, 40, 82, 88, 106–107, 115, 116

Peter Haigh, © Digital Vision: pp. 36–37, 66, 92–93, 112, 126

This book has been bound using
handcraft methods and
Smyth-sewn to ensure durability.

The dust jacket and interior were
designed by Corinda Cook.

The photos were researched
by Susan Oyama.

The text was edited by Molly Jay
and Joelle Herr.

The text was set in
Abadi and Veljovic.